WASHINGTON AND THE POET

By Francis Coleman Rosenberger

Washington and the Poet

EDITED BY

Francis Coleman Rosenberger

UNIVERSITY PRESS OF VIRGINIA

CHARLOTTESVILLE

Printed at The Stinehour Press and distributed by the University Press of Virginia, Box 3608, University Station, Charlottesville, Virginia 22903. Twelve hundred and fifty copies have been printed of which fifty copies are for the poets, six hundred copies are for members of the Columbia Historical Society and six hundred copies are for sale.

International Standard Book Number 0–8139–0753–5

Library of Congress Catalogue Card Number 77–81771

Contents

Preface

WASHINGTON, city and capital, has, from time to time, in one way or another, engaged the imagination of some of the best poets of my lifetime. This anthology is a gathering together of these Washington poems. The angle of vision of the poet will, I hope, intensify our own perception of the city.

There are many poets whose work has given me a good deal of pleasure who have never been moved to comment in verse on any aspect of the city. What this anthology shows is the remarkable thing that so many fine poets have written what may be called "a Washington poem." (There may well be others which, if I knew of them, I would have included.) The range and quality of the poems here are superior even to what I supposed was likely when I first began to assemble them. To bring them together has been a rewarding experience for me and I hope that to read them together may be a rewarding experience for others.

The anthology has been assembled largely through personal correspondence with the poets. I deeply appreciate the generous cooperation of the poets which alone has made the volume possible. Many of the poems have been published in individual volumes by their authors and these are noted in the copyright acknowledgements. Brief biographical and bibliographical notes on the poets appear at the end of the volume. The order of the poems here is chronological by the date of the birth of the poet.

Washington, Muriel Rukeyser's "City of Monuments," A. R. Ammons' "Marble," in Ernest Kroll's phrase "neither Rome nor home," is above all else, as it was designed to be, a city of government. But the poets may have the last word. As Archibald MacLeish wrote a long time ago in the poem with which the volume opens: "Have Gentlemen perhaps forgotten this?— / We write the histories."

Francis Coleman Rosenberger
Washington, D.C.
January 1977

Archibald MacLeish

A POET SPEAKS FROM THE VISITORS' GALLERY

Have Gentlemen perhaps forgotten this?—
We write the histories.

Do Gentlemen who snigger at the poets,
Who speak the word professor with guffaws—
Do Gentlemen expect their fame to flourish
When we, not they, distribute the applause?

Or do they trust their hope of long remembrance
To those they name with such respectful care—
To those who write the tittle in the papers,
To those who tell the tattle on the air?

Do Gentlemen expect the generation
That counts the losers out when tolls the bell
To take some gossip-caster's estimation,
Some junior voice of fame with fish to sell?

Do Gentlemen believe time's hard-boiled jury,
Judging the sober truth, will trust again
The words some copperhead who owned a paper
Ordered one Friday from the hired men?

Have Gentlemen forgotten Mr. Lincoln?

A poet wrote that story, not a newspaper,
Not the New Yorker of the nameless name
Who spat with hatred like some others later
And left, as they will, in his hate his shame.

History's not written in the kind of ink
The richest man of most ambitious mind
Who hates a president enough to print
A daily paper can afford or find.

1

Gentlemen have power now and know it,
But even the greatest and most famous kings
Feared and with reason to offend the poets
Whose songs are marble
                              and whose marble sings.

Horace Gregory

THE CHINESE GARDEN

Near the city of Washington, D.C., there is a Chinese Garden.
Few visit it; the place seems singularly deserted and remote.

O yes, the Chinese Garden! Do you remember
Sun beating behind clouds? One felt the air
Shaken by streams of yellow light through aether,
And yet late summer stillness in each turn
Of paths that ran between the fading grasses,
The well-deep, glassy pool, and the damp smell,
And clouded light around us everywhere—
The half-lit madness we can never cure.

You see them now! I mean the water lilies,
White petals open as a China cup
Rising above the surface of a tray:
They are here—just out of reach—and there, the water,
The half-light in far corners of the park,
Trees fallen around it through the pale arbutus.
Do you feel the grey light at the farthest clearing
Thrusting as snow against plate glass, then gone?

Beneath the cloud-white lilies, hairy roots,
Invisible lips that breathe the cool well water
Wavering in darkness down to dreamless sleep:
The streams to walk below the net of grasses
That close above the ripples of the soul.

There were no signs to warn us: "Walks ill-tended,
The bridges gone beneath the deeper grasses—"
Reach toward the lilies? Not that afternoon.
If one were tempted to lean out that far? . . .
No, no, not now! No one would dare to hear us.
"The water has turned black." We turned away:
It was like leaving a forbidden city,
Earth falling away behind us into darkness:
We heard a woman cry, "But O the flowers,
Where are the flowers? The beautiful white flowers!"

3

Allen Tate

AENEAS AT WASHINGTON

I myself saw furious with blood
Neoptolemus, at his side the black Atridae,
Hecuba and the hundred daughters, Priam
Cut down, his filth drenching the holy fires.
In that extremity I bore me well,
A true gentleman, valorous in arms,
Disinterested and honourable. Then fled:
That was a time when civilization
Run by the few fell to the many, and
Crashed to the shout of men, the clang of arms:
Cold victualing I seized, I hoisted up
The old man my father upon my back,
In the smoke made by sea for a new world
Saving little—a mind imperishable
If time is, a love of past things tenuous
As the hesitation of receding love.

(To the reduction of uncitied littorals
We brought chiefly the vigor of prophecy,
Our hunger breeding calculation
And fixed triumphs.)

                            I saw the thirsty dove
In the glowing fields of Troy, hemp ripening
And tawny corn, the thickening Blue Grass
All lying rich forever in the green sun.
I see all things apart, the towers that men
Contrive I too contrived long, long ago.
Now I demand little. The singular passion
Abides its object and consumes desire
In the circling shadow of its appetite.
There was a time when the young eyes were slow,
Their flame steady beyond the firstling fire,
I stood in the rain, far from home at nightfall

By the Potomac, the great Dome lit the water,
The city my blood had built I knew no more
While the screech-owl whistled his new delight
Consecutively dark.

                                       Stuck in the wet mire
Four thousand leagues from the ninth buried city
I thought of Troy, what we had built her for.

May Miller

THE WASHINGTONIAN

Possessed of this city, we are born
Into kinship with its people.
Eyes that looked upon
Cool magnificence of space,
The calm of marble,
And green converging on green
In long distances,
Bear their wonder to refute
Meaningless dimensions,
The Old-World facades.

The city is ours irrevocably
As pain sprouts at the edge of joy,
As grief grows large with our years.
New seeds push hard to topsoil;
Logic is a grafted flower
From roots in a changeless bed.
Skeleton steel may shadow the path,
Broken stone snag the foot,
But we shall walk again
Side by side with others on the street,
Each certain of his way home.

Ruth Lechlitner

A.B.S. NEWS

With morning coffee
(while a cloud smaller than a hand
prints headline weather)
I bow to the tube-shrine—the divinity
that protects us like a deodorant
from a possible human future;
to the whoremasters who put this pimp
atop the compost heap, to crow Truth
rare as a dusty mermaid.

Habit lends ear to his
daily oiled voice announcing
how yesterday's hounds still follow
footprints that vanish today
in black swamp water;
repeating last week's tale
of a virgin whose ripe womb held
her father's house; re-telling
the news of a millionaire's caper
(but not of the poet who slashed his wrists
and gave himself to Death . . .)

Now (climax!) that jawsome man with
the nose profile like a flag at half mast
—that chopstick and salty
summit travelling salesman
—that Noble Peace-sucker
whose (expletive) dangles between
bloody dollar sign prop-ups.
Commitment.

After this Message,
"Brand A zaps a headache
faster than B or C,"

shall I make it perfectly clear
that it's later than we think?

Except . . . except that there—
there beyond Arlington Bridge—
the memorial sculpture of greatness.
Those root-strong hands
still grasp (left and right)
the two arms of one nation:
that government by the people
shall not perish from the earth.

Lawrence Lee

THE DOME

If one's country is strong, one dreams it just
to its own citizens, as to all men;
with still unaltered nature, generous
even to the hostile and the envious.
They who by dream and action made
a largesse greater than had ever been
for spirit and mind,
for need and self-respect,
yet unafraid
remember that a people must
endlessly make its dreams again.

City where granite seems unfolding thought
and marble is a dream designed
that generations never shall neglect
the dreamer or the undreaming meek,
still seek,
though troubled still
with native and with alien ill,
that from the present time's bright capital
justice at last shall reach to all
and danger be less, or cease,
your grave enduring dome
become
a constant moon lighting a world at peace.

Katie Louchheim

PRIDE OF PLACE

Odd old woman named Georgetown
wrinkled face flowering
doorways lush-lavender
creeping wisteria,
tulips like soldiers
heirloom dogwood pink lace
bowed branch weeping cherry
repent pride, spring's surprise.

Worn stoops overpriced,
dark brick-stitched empires
hounded by tourists, by trash.
Curious curtains forgive
dog's manners, tight jeans,
small cars parked, couples
late in black-tied haste
reason, lesser human treasons.

Brewster Ghiselin

ROULETTE

We will not withdraw from the game.

We can win at the next. . . . Who knows?

And we dare not say to our dead,
"We fail you, now you are dead,
As then—before you died."

Let the statesman hold up his head!
Let him not flinch from the click
As the empty chamber shifts.

Statesmen hold up their heads.

A hot revolver lifting
Loaded to the full, every chamber
Charged to fire, FIRES—

But is pointing away from us,
Turning, pointing to the temple
Of another, of others, the others.

The gun-shy are dying, far off.

Statesmen hold up their heads.

Statesmen hold up our heads.

Richard Eberhart

THE GODS OF WASHINGTON, D.C.

I was wondering about the gods
As I was walking down Constitution Avenue
For always since I was a boy
I was conscious of the gods in the offing,

Always off there somewhere in the air,
Never immediate and satisfactory,
Yet indubitably the master stuff
And living and seeing of our being,

And now here on Constitution Avenue,
With memorial buildings austere and white,
I wondered about the gods of the world,
Their existence, their glory, and their authority.

The gods were so plural and so vague,
Yet so powerful and so composite
That I was perplexed on Constitution Avenue
Even as I had been perplexed as a boy

And nurture this poem about the gods,
Who spring and leap out of our blood,
As one still seeking for definition
At odds with, but admitting the gods

And if they were a fallacy or illusion
May they go back before their birth,
But if they are a waking fact and a conclusion
May they state their case and return

For in this century of delicate balance
We have need of the gods of the air,
Stout gods, stubborn as bony man,
But we ought to know whether they are there.

Robert Penn Warren

PATRIOTIC TOUR AND POSTULATE OF JOY

Once, once, in Washington,
D.C., in June,
All night—I swear it—a single mockingbird
Sang,
Sang to the Presidential ear,
Wherein it poured
Such criticism and advice as that ear
Had rarely had the privilege to hear.

And sang to every senator
Available,
And some, as sources best informed affirm,
Rose,
Rose with a taste in the throat like bile,
To the bathroom fled
And spat, and faced the mirror there, and while
The bicarb fizzed, stared, feet cold on tile.

And sang to Edgar Hoover, too,
And as it preached
Subversion and all bright disaster, he
Woke;
Woke, then looked at Mom's photo, so heard
No more. But far,
Far off in Arlington, the heroes stirred
And meditated on the message of that bird.

And sang—oh, merciless!—to me,
Who to that place
And to that massive hour had moved, and now
Rose,
Rose naked, and shivered in moonlight, and cried
Out in my need
To know what postulate of joy men have tried
To live by, in sunlight and moonlight, until they died.

Stanley Kunitz

FOREIGN AFFAIRS

We are two countries girded for the war,
Whisking our scouts across the pricked frontier
To ravage in each other's fields, cut lines
Along the lacework of strategic nerves,
Loot stores; while here and there,
In ambushes that trace a valley's curves,
Stark witness to the dangerous charge we bear,
A house ignites, a train's derailed, a bridge
Blows up sky-high, and water floods the mines.
Who first attacked? Who turned the other cheek?
Aggression perpetrated is as soon
Denied, and insult rubbed into the injury
By cunning agents trained in these affairs,
With whom it's touch-and-go, don't-tread-on-me,
I-dare-you-to, keep-off, and kiss-my-hand.
Tempers could sharpen knives, and do; we live
In states provocative
Where frowning headlines scare the coffee cream
And doomsday is the eighth day of the week.

Our exit through the slammed and final door
Is twenty times rehearsed, but when we face
The imminence of cataclysmic rupture,
A lesser pride goes down upon its knees.
Two countries separated by desire!—
Whose diplomats speed back and forth by plane,
Portmanteaus stuffed with fresh apologies
Outdated by events before they land.
Negotiations wear them out: they're driven mad
Between the protocols of tears and rapture.

Locked in our fated and contiguous selves,
These worlds that too much agitate each other,
Interdependencies from hip to head,

Twin principalities both slave and free,
We coexist, proclaiming Peace together.
Tell me no lies! We are divided nations
With malcontents by thousands in our streets,
These thousands torn by inbred revolutions.
A triumph is demanded, not moral victories
Deduced from small advances, small retreats.
Are the gods of our fathers not still daemonic?
On the steps of the Capitol
The outraged lion of our years roars panic,
And we suffer the guilty cowardice of the will,
Gathering its bankrupt slogans up for flight
Like gold from ruined treasuries.
And yet, and yet, although the murmur rises,
We are what we are, and only life surprises.

Josephine Jacobsen

NIGHT PATROL

(Washington)

The wolf's cousin
then gentled to clown for us,
paces now, forbidden
to be trusted, or trust:
paces the pavement.

The black shoes and the furry toes
pace together on the wide
night street; from the raw light pace
into the jungle of shadows.
The wolf blood courses under hide.
The feet echo; silent go the paws.

A clock strikes winter.
Hunters are cold as hunted.
The dog teaches the man to listen:
something waits in the shadows' center.
The wolf heart knows what is wanted,
called back from a dream unnatural and human.

They walked like mutant friends, in a season's sun;
now they walk like wolves, and know their own.
Their own move toward them: empty, the street
moves toward them, where in this bitter season
cold wolf and wolf meet.

Selden Rodman

I DREAMED THAT WASHINGTON LAY
WREATHED IN SMOKE

August 6, 1945: Hiroshima

I dreamed that Washington lay wreathed in smoke,
Steaming with poisons as a stagnant lake,
And honeycombed, like Nuremberg, with tunnels
Through which the people crawled. The darkest channels
Converged in spokes upon a hollow center,
And I was leading a conducted tour
Down the inverted Monument, whose tip
Pointed to hell. I knew it was a trap
But still went on. The air grew thick and stank
And as we neared the midden's very brink
I saw a monstrous Thing. Its face was hidden.
Yet I knew at once it was the Iron Maiden,
And started back in horror. But the crowd
Seized me, and tied my arms against my side,
And laughing, tore away the iron shirt
And pushed me in to be her beating heart.
I was too terrified to resist, too weak
To scream. And as the spiked doors closed, I woke.

Elizabeth Bishop

VIEW OF THE CAPITOL
FROM THE LIBRARY OF CONGRESS

Moving from left to left, the light
is heavy on the Dome, and coarse.
One small lunette turns it aside
and blankly stares off to the side
like a big white old wall-eyed horse.

On the east steps the Air Force Band
in uniforms of Air Force blue
is playing hard and loud, but—queer—
the music doesn't quite come through.

It comes in snatches, dim then keen,
then mute, and yet there is no breeze.
The giant trees stand in between.
I think the trees must intervene,

catching the music in their leaves
like gold-dust, till each big leaf sags.
Unceasingly the little flags
feed their limp stripes into the air,
and the band's efforts vanish there.

Great shades, edge over,
give the music room.
The gathered brasses want to go
boom—boom.

Josephine Miles

SOFTLY THE CAPITOL HILL SURVEYS ITS SCENE

Softly the capitol hill surveys its scene,
The roads of its marble caverns
On which it governs,
Litter of tombs.

Each stone figure put to sitting
Upon his grave
Faces outward, skyward and sunward,
Thinking to live.

Underground, whoo, whoo, something is coming,
That's the ticket,
Straight up the aisle breaking the silence
Dirt flies out of the railway tunnel.

On the other side of the track and valley
Tracking his hole,
The old mole is busy upchucking
A new hill.

We will build up the hill and come up so the white of the eye
Will be lambent and clear
At our height and will look to us level
And straight as we near.

And the word will be *lawmaking*, made for us here as we stand
Not back home, not below, not down under,
But ready
And here at your hand.

Robert Hayden

THE PEACOCK ROOM

in memory of Betsy Graves Reyneau

Ars Longa   Which is crueller
Vita Brevis   life or art?
          Thoughts in the Peacock Room,
where briefly I shelter. As in the glow
(remembered or imagined?)
          of the lamp shaped like a rose
my mother would light
for me some nights to keep
          Raw-Head-And-Bloody-Bones away.

Exotic, fin de siècle, unreal
and beautiful the Peacock Room.
          Triste metaphor.
Hiroshima   Watts   My Lai.
Thus history scorns
          the vision chambered in gold
and Spanish leather, lyric space;
rebukes, yet cannot give the lie
          to what is havened here.

Environment as ornament.
Whistler with arrogant art designed
          it, mocking a connoisseur
with satiric arabesque of gold
peacocks on a wall peacock blue
          in fury trampling coins of gold.
Such vengeful harmonies drove
a rival mad. As in a dream
          I see the crazed young man.

He shudders in a corner, shields
his face in terror of
          the perfect malice of those claws.

She too is here—ghost
of the happy child she was that day.
     When I turned twelve,
they gave me for a birthday gift
a party in the Peacock Room.
     With shadow cries

the peacocks flutter down,
their spread tails concealing her,
     then folding, drooping to reveal
her eyeless, old—Med School
cadaver, flesh-object
     pickled in formaldehyde,
who was artist, compassionate,
clear-eyed. Who was belovèd friend.
     No more. No more.

The birds resume their splendored pose.
And Whistler's portrait of
     a tycoon's daughter gleams
like imagined flowers. What is art?
What is life?
     What the Peacock Room?
Rose-leaves and ashes drift
its portals, gently spinning toward
     a bronze Bodhisattva's ancient smile.

Karl Shapiro

WASHINGTON CATHEDRAL

From summer and the wheel-shaped city
    That sweats like a swamp and wrangles on
    Its melting streets, white mammoth Forums,
And political hotels with awnings, caryatids;
Past barricaded embassies with trees
    That shed trash and parch his eyes,
To here, the acres of superior quiet,
    Shadow and damp, the tourist comes,
    And, cooled by stones and darkness, stares.

Tall as a lover's night, the nave
    Broods over him, irradiates,
And stars of color out of painted glass
Shoot downward on apostles and on chairs
Huddled by hundreds under altar rails.
Yet it is only Thursday; there are no prayers,

But exclamations. The lady invokes by name
    The thousand-odd small sculptures, spooks,
    New angels, pitted roods; she gives
The inventory of relics to his heart
That aches with history and astonishment:
He gives a large coin to a wooden coffer.

Outside, noon blazes in his face like guns.
He goes down by the Bishop's walk, the dial,
    The expensive grass, the Byzantine bench,
While stark behind him a red naked crane
    Hangs over the unfinished transept,
A Cubist hen rivalling the Gothic School.

Whether he sees the joke; whether he cares;
Whether he tempts a vulgar miracle,
Some deus ex machina, this is his choice,

A shrine of whispers and tricky penumbras.
    Therefore he votes again for the paid
Clergy, the English hint, the bones of Wilson
Crushed under tons of fake magnificence.
    Nor from the zoo of his instincts
    Come better than crude eagles: now
He cannot doubt that violent obelisk
And Lincoln whittled to a fool's colossus.
This church and city triumph in his eyes.
He is only a good alien, nominally happy.

Muriel Rukeyser

CITY OF MONUMENTS
Washington 1934

Be proud   you people   of these graves
    these chiseled words   this precedent
From these blind ruins shines our monument.

Dead navies of the brain will sail
    stone celebrate its final choice
    when the air shakes, a single voice
a strong voice able to prevail   :

Entrust no hope to stone although the stone
shelter the root   :   see too-great burdens placed
with nothing certain but the risk
set on the infirm column of
the high memorial obelisk

erect in accusation sprung against
a barren sky taut over Anacostia   :
give over, Gettysburg   !   a word will shake your glory   :
blood of the starved fell thin upon this plain,
this battle is not buried with its slain.

    Gravestone and battlefield retire
    the whole green South is shadowed dark,
    the slick white domes are cast in night.
    But uneclipsed above the park

    the veteran of the Civil War
    sees havoc in the tended graves
    the midnight bugles blown to free
    still unemancipated slaves.

Blinded by chromium or transfiguration
we watch, as through a microscope, decay   :
   down the broad streets the limousines
advance in passions of display.

Air glints with diamonds, and these clavicles
emerge through orchids by whose trailing spoor
the sensitive cannot mistake
the implicit anguish of the poor.

The throats incline, the marble men rejoice
careless of torrents of despair.

Split by a tendril of revolt
stone cedes to blossom everywhere.

William Stafford

HERO

What if he came back, astounded
to find his name so honored, schools
named after him, a flame at his tomb,
his careless words cherished? How could
he ever face the people again, knowing
all he would know in that great clarity
of the other side? (His eyes flare into
the eyes of his wife. He searches his brother's
drawn face turned toward him suddenly still.)

No. Better abandoned in the ground
recklessly cast back into the trash of
our atoms, all once loved let languish:
a lost civilization loses by particulars,
faith eroded by faithlessly treating
its servants. (Remember the slippering
progress the hearse made?—dwindling importantly
where faces could never really turn round?)

Our words apologize for such chill,
engulfing perspectives. We look deep into
the branded time helplessly and then come
chattering back for assurance, to shore up
our relics: *Arma virumque cano*. Such effort
it takes to build the high walls of Rome.

Randall Jarrell

THE WOMAN AT THE WASHINGTON ZOO

The saris go by me from the embassies.

Cloth from the moon. Cloth from another planet.
They look back at the leopard like the leopard.

And I. . . .
                         this print of mine, that has kept its color
Alive through so many cleanings; this dull null
Navy I wear to work, and wear from work, and so
To my bed, so to my grave, with no
Complaints, no comment: neither from my chief,
The Deputy Chief Assistant, nor his chief—
Only I complain. . . . this serviceable
Body that no sunlight dyes, no hand suffuses
But, dome-shadowed, withering among columns,
Wavy beneath fountains—small, far-off, shining
In the eyes of animals, these beings trapped
As I am trapped but not, themselves, the trap,
Aging, but without knowledge of their age,
Kept safe here, knowing not of death, for death—
Oh, bars of my own body, open, open!

The world goes by my cage and never sees me.
And there come not to me, as come to these,
The wild beasts, sparrows pecking the llamas' grain,
Pigeons settling on the bears' bread, buzzards
Tearing the meat the flies have clouded. . . .
                                        Vulture,
When you come for the white rat that the foxes left,
Take off the red helmet of your head, the black
Wings that have shadowed me, and step to me as man:
The wild brother at whose feet the white wolves fawn,
To whose hand of power the great lioness
Stalks, purring. . . .
                     You know what I was,
You see what I am: change me, change me!

27

John Berryman

DREAM SONG 200

I am interested & amazed: on the building across the way
from where I vaguely live there are no bars!
Best-looking place in town.
Only them lawyers big with great cigars
and lesser with briefcases, instead of minds,
move calmly in & out

and now or then an official limousine
with a live Supreme Court justice & chauffeur
mounts the ramp toward me.
We live *behind*, you see. It's Christmas, and *brrr*
in Washington. My wife's candle is out
for John F. Kennedy

and the law rushes like mud but the park is white
with a heavy fall for ofays & for dark,
let's exchange blue-black kisses
for the fate of the Man who was not born today,
clashing our tinsel, by the terrible tree
whereon he really hung, for you & me.

Ernest Kroll

WASHINGTON, D.C.

Hearing the twang among the porticoes
Where one expected only noble Romans,
You turn and keep a mild surprise, seeing
The public man descend the marble stairs,
Yourself, but for the grace of God, in the blue day
Among the floating domes. He disappears,
A little heady in that atmosphere,
Trailing the air of power, a solemn figure
Quick in the abstract landscape of the state.
His passage leaves you baffled in the void,
Looking out between two columns. The sun
Burns in the silence of the white façades.

How shall you act the natural man in this
Invented city, neither Rome nor home?

Francis Coleman Rosenberger

A MEMORIAL FOR MR. JEFFERSON

The white marble squats among the mosquitos
And Mr. Jefferson is not here.
The monstrous Jefferson, like papier-mâché,
Three times life, leans from the Potomac
And the poll tax.

The Jacobin shadow falls
Upon the picnickers and their Sunday boats.
Buried under the columns, the masonry,
Is the dream of fitting government
And the happy state.

This does you no service, good citizen
Who drew your own so modest monument.
Your words, chosen as carefully as the boxwood,
Buttress the memorial where Mr. Smith
May lay his wreath.

The interior, domed, and the portico,
The plaza, the house in caricature:
Here once more is the silly Browere
Striking the features of the face
That he would keep.

Washington 1945

Edward Weismiller

JUST ASK FOR A DEMONSTRATION

1.

I told the White House I wanted to write a poem.
At first there was no answer, no sound
As of dust falling, or a nail pulling, or a chair scraping.
Then a voice said, "Do you have to?"

                                 "Oh, yes," I said.

"Why?"

             "I have to tell you the way I feel."
"Is it the way I feel?"

                    "I don't think so.
             That's the point."
"I like to listen to people who are dead
Who made me feel the way I do. Not many
Writers can write that well."

                     "I—I guess not."
"Well, good to talk with you. Good—."

                          "Wait. I mean—."
"I'm very busy."

                 "I know. Excuse me. Those writers—."
"Shakespeare. Robert W. Service. Like that."
"How do you know what people feel like now?"
"I listen to people who feel the way I do
But are too shy to tell me so."

                 "I see. Well
Just the same I'd like to—. It's important
To me to—. It's the way being a poet
Is—."

The voice said, "The artists of our country,
All but a small, vocal minority,
Are the finest in the world, and we want the world
To know that we're proud of their awareness, that we
Have faith in them. . . . Do you have to?"

2.

I said, "I want this poem
To be the best I ever wrote. To mean the most."
"When were you thinking of writing it?" a voice said.
"Now. Well, any time. When would it work out for you—?"
"Say in a few weeks? You can have the Monument grounds."
"But how could you hear, that far? And I was wanting
To tell you the way I feel right now."

                                  "I'm sure
Mature reflection—."
                     "Pennsylvania Avenue?
Right outside the White House? So you can hear,
Because it's you I want to know the shape
Of what I'm thinking—."
                       "You understand, the President
Can't take on every job. But someone—
Julie and David; someone. . . . A month from now, then;
The Monument grounds. By the way, can you guarantee
That there won't be any violence? We can't have violence."
"I'll do my best. I don't want any either,
But words—when you start putting words together—.
All I can say is I'm not planning any.
I can control—."
                  "We'll have to take precautions."

3.

A month went by. I said to a high official
On the White House staff, "I'm writing my poem."
He didn't have to tell me no one was listening.
That night I dreamed a poem that burned the town.

Eugene McCarthy

DULLES AIRPORT

Detached by Saarinen or God
from all coordinates,
it sits like a gull upon water
defying the subtle archimedean rule.

The earth flows without displacement.
In this the only measured space of the world,
we come each a half two hundred yards
from shadow to form
from form to person, to meet
within the green range of each other's sight.

There at the center point, at midnight,
no arrivals, or departures scheduled
ticket sellers and stewardesses sleep,
planes and pilots are released.

Into this innocence of light,
not one eye of the myriad-eyed mankind
dares look. Let us dance, slowly turning.
We are seen by the immodest,
unlidded, unblinking, snaked-eyed electric beam.
The door opens out. Not driven
but drawn by darkness, we go
naked into the immeasurable night.

Charles Edward Eaton

THE LAST PAGE BUT ONE

There will come a day when you will remember History all too well.
The deaths of kings and princes, shady politics at home,
Cleopatra and her asp and why the Bastille fell.

You will, for once, look the American Eagle in the eyes,
And feel his vast, impersonal, amber stare
As though you cannot know too much and still be counted wise.

Somewhere, perhaps in sleep, you stroked the lion's mane
And sensed the heavy, heavy coursing blood of time
As it asserts its massive way through every sensual vein.

And you will ask yourself as you accelerate the brute intake
Of classic myths relived without a sense of form
If this could be by any chance the summer of the last heartbreak.

You will be bold enough to stand as on an autumn plain,
For autumn seems, in fact, to be the meat of History's mood,
And, in advance, relume the summer as one that will not come again.

In such a light the step beyond is calculated risk—
Awakening the lion, flushing the bird, keeping the angry doors
    wide open,
You never let the heart remind it is not equal to the task.

John Malcolm Brinnin

BIRD TALK

I knew a man kept a yellow bird
in a little cage red, white and blue.
"Listen!" he said. "*Where* have you heard
a tone so pure, a pitch so true?"

"Bel canto . . ." I said. "What sweet high C's!
Clearly those notes are just for you."
The yellow bird bowed, hopped his trapeze,
and shivered the air with all he knew.

"Nighty night," said the man, and drew a shawl
on that little house of bright bamboo.
"Such virtue," he sighed, "in a thing so small."
Yuk foo, sang the bird, yuk foo, yuk foo.

Charles G. Bell

APPROACHING WASHINGTON

Lights, along the tidal reaches
Dark – cities – I see you lovelier
And lonelier than ever in our days
Of hope, your beauty rooted
In your loneliness.

Dark by day, clouding
The embayments of your streams,
Breeding hutches of our troubled souls,
At night you constellate a coil of flame
Along the roads of water.

And we, airborne, at night
Take by the bay the renewed
Dragon of fire. The old snake
Casts his skin; and every scale
Glints spangled in our tears.

Robert Lowell

JULY IN WASHINGTON

The stiff spokes of this wheel
touch the sore spots of the earth.

On the Potomac, swan-white
power launches keep breasting the sulphurous wave.

Otters slide and dive and slick back their hair,
raccoons clean their meat in the creek.

On the circles, green statues ride like South American
liberators above the breeding vegetation—

prongs and spearheads of some equatorial
backland that will inherit the globe.

The elect, the elected . . . they come here bright as dimes,
and die disheveled and soft.

We cannot name their names, or number their dates—
circle on circle, like rings on a tree—

but we wish the river had another shore,
some farther range of delectable mountains,

distant hills powdered blue as a girl's eyelid.
It seems the least little shove would land us there,

that only the slightest repugnance of our bodies
we no longer control could drag us back.

Radcliffe Squires

A MARCH ON WASHINGTON

for the Union and Confederate Dead

Those black planes, whose speed makes silent air
Clap hands, seem to move now in the vast canary
Of the winter sunset as slowly as the stars
And flocks of birds that are also moving there
Dumbly, their definition lost in a yellow light
That is, like madness, too definite.

I pull my eyes from the window
And back to the striated, guitar-string icons
Of television where in the city of Washington
That poet—who wherever he turns smells brimstone—
Stands before his army of the helpless young.
They smile as he speaks, but he is not
Really speaking to them. His words go out
To the lady of history, that whore who muses
With Rubicon lips on her silken bed, who chooses
Only to hear what was never said,
Though she smiles to encourage the poet's words:
"You are so beautiful, lady, why can't you also be good?"

Be good, be good. She has not heard.
But I think someone has. Some small boy
Hears and gently gives up his toys.
From this moment on he will not bother
With thoughts of crawling back into mother
Or diddling sister or poisoning father
Or any of the fantasies usual and small
Which in the long run make people slightly bearable.
His followers, even now bored with mechano sets,
Are calmly waiting for him to say, "What
We must do to our brothers is wrong except it is good."

The poet's face suddenly races up the screen,
Disappears and reappears at the bottom line,
Jerks like an acrobat up the guitar strings.
The static shadow sprints backward in the seething stream.

I glance again at the window. The planes seem
Scarcely to have moved. Like snails
They leave on the sky a pearly trail.

William Jay Smith

THE RISE AND FALL OF THE SWAGGER STICK

I

Gen. Lemuel C. Shepherd Jr. (the new Marine Corps Comman-
dant) has issued an order that "all male officers are authorized and
encouraged" to carry swagger sticks when not actually bearing
arms.   —Washington, United Press, 1954

When things in Washington get thick
The answer is the swagger stick.
In other days of public swagger,
We had the rapier and the dagger.
Officers could then advance
With the halberd or the lance,
With the bilbo or the skean,
Or the stylet damascene,
Whose blade is sure and quick and clean.
None today is politic:
Orderly, my swagger stick!

II

Gen. David M. Shoup (the new Marine Corps Commandant)
. . . gave this advice to members of the corps: ". . . be aggressive,
visionary, persistent, and timely. . . . There is one item of equip-
ment about which I have a definite opinion. . . . It is the swagger
stick. It shall remain an optional item of interference. If you feel
the need of it, carry it." No marine in Washington has been seen
with a swagger stick since the commandant gave his talk.
                              —Washington, *N. Y. Times*, 1960

When things in Washington get thick,
The answer is *no* swagger stick.
Shoup has given meager clearance
To this article of interference.
Be visionary and aggressive,

Timely, and not retrogressive.
Do not flutter, don't get flustered,
Click your heels, and cut the mustard.
Persist or else, you bare-faced bustard.
Orderly, dust me off that brick,
And put away my swagger stick!

William Meredith

A MILD-SPOKEN CITIZEN FINALLY WRITES TO THE WHITE HOUSE

Please read this letter when you are alone.
Don't be afraid to listen to what may change you,
I am urging on you only what I myself have done.

In the first place, I respect the office, although one night
last spring, when you had committed (in my eyes)
criminal folly, and there was a toast to you, I wouldn't rise.

A man's mistakes (if I may lecture you), his worst acts,
aren't out of character, as he'd like to think,
are not put on him by power or stress or too much to drink,

but are simply a worse self he consents to be. Thus
there is no mistaking you. I marvel that there's
so much disrespect for a man just being himself, being his errors.

"I never met a worse man than myself,"
Thoreau said. When we're our best selves, we can all
afford to say that. Self-respect is best when marginal.

And when the office of the presidency will again
accommodate that remark (Did you see? Fidel Castro
said almost that recently) it may be held by better men

than you or me. Meantime, I hear there is music in your house,
your women wear queens' wear, though winds howl outside,
and I say, that's all right, the man should have some ease,

but does anyone say to your face who you really are?
No, they say *Mr. President*, while any young person
feels free to call me *voter*, *believer*, even *causer*.

And if I were also a pray-er, a man given to praying,
(I'm often in fact careless about great things, like you)
and I wanted to pray for your office, as in fact I do,

the words that would come to me would more likely be
god change you than *god bless the presidency,*
I would pray, *God cause the President to change.*

As I myself have been changed, first my head, then my heart,
so that I no longer pretend that I don't swindle or kill
when there is swindling and killing on my nation's part.

Well. Go out into your upstairs hall tonight with this letter.
Generous ghosts must walk that house at night,
carrying draughts of the Republic like cold water

to a man parched after too much talk and wine and smoke.
Hear them. They are elected ghosts, though some will be radicals
and all may want to tell you things you will not like.

It will seem dark in the carpeted hall, despite the night-lights
in the dull sconces. Make the guard let you pass.
"If you are the President," a shade with a water-glass

will ask you (and this is all I ask), calling you by name,
himself perhaps a famous name, "If you are the President,
and things in the land have come to all this shame,

why don't you try doing something new? This building rose,
laborious as a dream, to house one character:
man trusting man anew. That's who each tenant is

—or an impostor, as some of us have been."
                                                                1971

Reed Whittemore

WASHINGTON INTERREGNUM

When politicos of the old life have departed,
Movers enter,
And painters,
And sometimes fumigators,
To help get the new life started.

In the halls there are boxes and echoes.
There is rain on windows.
Inside windows,
Framed by taxpayers' marble,
An occasional lingering face in its lostness mellows.

Newcomers straggle up and down in the wet
Waiting, uneasily dressy, on alien corners,
Calling for taxis,
Searching out parties,
Questing for something obscure, unnamed, unmet.

The something decided not to attend the Ball,
Nor grace the Parade.
It failed to appear and perform in the grandstand charade
On the Hill.
Maybe it hides in an old box in a hall?

Maybe not. Anyway, there are offices, empty.
There is rain.
There is marble.
There are also the rust and ruin of parting pleasantry.
And there is the smell of new paint, in all the empty.

John Pauker

THE POET IN WASHINGTON

The ills of a poet are dull and routine affairs
Neglect, misunderstanding.
To liven his life, let's kick the poet downstairs
And hear his head crunch on the landing.

Howard Nemerov

Each morning when I break my buttered toast
Across the columns of the *Morning Post*,
I am astounded by the ways in which
Mankind has managed once again to bitch
Things up to a degree that yesterday
Had looked impossible. Not far away
From dreams of mine, I read this dream of theirs,
And think: It's true, we *are* the bankrupt heirs
Of all the ages, history *is* the bunk.
If you do not believe in all this junk,
If you're not glad things are not as they are,
    You can wipe your arse on the *Evening Star*.

Richard Wilbur

A MILTONIC SONNET FOR MR. JOHNSON
ON HIS REFUSAL OF PETER HURD'S OFFICIAL PORTRAIT

Heir to the office of a man not dead
Who drew our Declaration up, who planned
Range and Rotunda with his drawing-hand
And harbored Palestrina in his head,
Who would have wept to see small nations dread
The imposition of our cattle-brand,
With public truth at home mistold or banned,
And in whose term no army's blood was shed,

Rightly you say the picture is too large
Which Peter Hurd by your appointment drew,
And justly call that Capitol too bright
Which signifies our people in your charge;
Wait, Sir, and see how time will render you,
Who talk of vision but are weak of sight.

6 January 1967

Louis Simpson

BIG DREAM, LITTLE DREAM

The Elgonyi say, there are big dreams and little dreams.
The little dream is just personal. . . .
Sitting in a plane that is flying
too close to the ground. There are wires . . .
on either side there's a wall.

The big dream feels significant.
The big dream is the kind the president has.
He wakes and tells it to the secretary,
together they tell it to the cabinet,
and before you know there is war.

Maxine Kumin

MY HORSE, AMANDA:
THE SUMMER OF THE WATERGATE HEARINGS

I wake in New Hampshire.
The sun is still withheld.
For six days Amanda has stood
through drizzles and downpours.

This morning she steams.
Little pyramids of her droppings
surround her. Dead worms
shine in them like forgotten

spaghetti, proof she has eaten
the sugar-coated cure.
Four dozen ascarids, ten strongyles—
I count them to make sure.

And all the while in Washington
worms fall out of the government
pale as the parasites that drain
from the scoured gut of my mare.

They blink open on the television screen.
Night after night on the rerun
I count them to make sure.

A. R. Ammons

MARBLE

Never did get down there to Washington:
but course I heard tell of the place:
I met a feller once who'd been there
hisself: said he had: he said the main
thing about it was that whichever way you
went you got lost, them round squares with
gen'als pointing pistols and swords the wrong
way: feller said what they call a public

servant there's got servants, terrible
big cars, and doodads: said you couldn't
tell for sure if you'd orter speak to one
of them—anyway, couldn't find out where
any of them was: just think, I said to
this feller, live your whole life and never
see a president: course I heard from

the president: he sent for Luke, you remember
Luke: and then every year I send down
there whatever I got clear: sometimes
I think maybe I don't even live in this
country or Washington ain't in the country,
one: it gets pretty fuzzy: but the Bible
talks about kings and Nineveh: I reckon
I know more about Nineveh than Washington.

Robert Bly

AT A MARCH AGAINST THE
VIETNAM WAR

Washington, November 27, 1965

Newspapers rise high in the air over Maryland

We walk about, bundled in coats
    and sweaters in the late November sun

Looking down, I see feet moving
Calmly, gaily,
Almost as if separated from their bodies

But there is something moving in the dark somewhere
Just beyond
The edge of our eyes: a boat
Covered with machine guns
Moving along under trees

It is black,
The hand reaches out
And cannot touch it—
It is that darkness among pine boughs
That the Puritans brushed
As they went out to kill turkeys

At the edge of the jungle clearing
It explodes
On the ground

We long to abase ourselves

We have carried around this cup of darkness
We have longed to pour it over our heads

We make war
Like a man anointing himself

Roderick Jellema

WASHINGTON MIGRANTS

Birds obeying migration maps etched in their brains
never revise their interstate routes.
Some of them still stop off in Washington, D.C.

As the lights of the Pentagon probe this autumn dusk,
a peaceful V-sign of Canada geese lower their landing gear,
slip on the oily Potomac, break rank and huddle

among power boats. Wings of jets beat the air, taking turns
for the landing—pterodactyls circling the filled-in swamps
under National Airport. There is a great wild honking

of traffic on the bridges—
the daily homing of migrants with headlights dimmed
who loop and bank by instinct along broken white lines.

O. B. Hardison

PRO MUSICA ANTIQUA

after a performance at the Kennedy Center, April 5, 1974

Listen to the music.
Listen to the sound of the krumhorn, the rebeck,
The vielle, the virginal, the viola da gamba,
The scraping and twanging celebration of order.
It is all in the best possible order.
It streams up through the air of your house
And it is like summer,
A kind of sunlight slanting through the dust
Of almost empty air.

Throw away the dictionary.
Live where you are.
If the sackbut palls,
Bang on a pianoforte.
Limber up the drums,
Unleash saxophones, let everything run wild.
Have voices, too, whole masses of voices,
Doing the Niebelungenlied by ear.

This is the way it should be. Your house should be music.
Welcome it, hold on to it, sweat, let it pour into you
Like an old god making demigods with mortals.
Hold on until your every motion is dance.
Having received, enlarge.
When you let go, you will snore in C major.

Robert Dana

THE WATERGATE ELEGY

Justice corrupts

All those years of spying
years of fear
The cold tit of the Capitol

No man can afford to lose his best enemies

The White House white as cake
there must have been months
when whole Mafias of black limousine kissed the curb
drab captains debouching with report
lieutenants packing heavy info

And out of New Jersey through Mexico
Out of the Florida Keys
Out of San Clemente to Angel City
what couriers ferrying tropical memoranda
what sugars carried for silence

The politic is power
suspicion the currency of its hunger
lies property to be kept safe under combinations

Sicken waters
Die land
And if the citizen eat his rights for bread and meat
in such least light
the kept counsels prosper

Spring is long gone from this city
The mallards
shackled to their Potomac slough in a surprise of ice
waiting for the sun to warm
They too are gone

This city is not a wheel for nothing
not white for nothing amid its blacks and cherry trees

But the axle is broken
the hub empty

And at the end of his reflection
Lincoln shrinks into the dark memorial of his penny

Gary Snyder

Far above the dome
Of the capitol—
It's true!
A large bird soars
Against white cloud,
Wings arced,
Sailing easy in this
Humid southern sun-blurred
   breeze—
 the dark-suited policeman
 watches tourist cars—
And the center,
The center of power is nothing!
Nothing here.
Old white stone domes,
Strangely quiet people,

Earth-sky-bird patterns
 idly interlacing

The world does what it pleases.

Linda Pastan

BICENTENNIAL WINTER

The only revolution is among the oaks
here in the woods;
their mutinous leaves
refuse to fall, despite
the laws of season
and of gravity.
Red-coated cardinals hide
among those leaves.
Red bird, cold weather
the farmers say.
Know us by our myths.
I think of the mutinous
Puritans who taught us
that all things break.
We have forgotten that,
disenchanted;
amazed as children told
for the first time
how they were conceived.
Still the mind moves
continually west, following
paths beaten by the sun
risking ambush
and early darkness.
On Sundays, driving
past frontiers
lit by milkweed
let us find what wilderness
is left. Deep in the woods
it's possible to see the cruelties
between fox and rabbit
and their mutual beauty;
to study the creeks:
how the citizenry of small stones

is washed in waters that run
to the Potomac,
still clear in places,
in places muddy.
Today the river's a frozen slate,
a tabula rasa. It tempts us
as it did two hundred winters ago
to dare the dangerous
freedom
of the skater.

Grace Cavalieri

TO THE PRESIDENT CROSSING THE POTOMAC, 1977

In crossing the Potomac, think twice before arriving,
Being sure that incidents connect,
Crucial work is written; Trifles succeed instead

Our river is from the eyes of men

Prizes of learning on paper show
A subtle breakage.
I see strange things,
Jackets outgrown,
Cellars abandoned,
Orchards dead of trees,
Memories of poems,
A year of ash.

Imperfect lengths of measure bring it together,
The fair and the quiet, here

And reason to begin again

In your chamber, hearing hits. Death waits,
Care and find. Tomorrow we will quote phrases
Of harmony and truth concealing blossoms from the jaw

The past embraces,
Large feelings like blue climb and
The sleeping lie here like seeds
In fierce flashing for your memory.

June Jordan

POEM: ON MORAL LEADERSHIP AS A POLITICAL DILEMMA

Watergate, 1973

I don't know why but
I cannot tell a lie

I chopped down the cherry tree
I did
I did that
yessirree
I chopped down the cherry tree

and to tell you the truth
see
that was only in the morning

which left a whole day and part
of an evening (until suppertime)
to continue doing what I like to do

about cherry trees

which is

to chop them down

then pick the cherries
and roll them into a cherry-pie circle
and then
stomp the cherries
stomp them
jumping up and down
hard and heavy
jumping up to stomp them
so the flesh leaks and the juice
runs loose

and then I get to pick at the pits
or else I pick up the cherry pits
(depending on my mood)
and then
I fill my mouth completely full
of cherry pits
and run over to the river
the Potomac
where I spit
47 to 65 cherry pits spit
into the Potomac
at one spit

and to tell you the truth some more
if I ever see a cherry tree
standing around no matter where
and here let me please be perfectly clear
no matter where
I see a cherry tree
standing around

even if it belongs to a middle-American of
moderate means with a two-car family
that is falling apart in a respectable
civilized
falling apart
mind-your-manners manner

even then

or even if you happen to be
corporate rich or
unspeakably poor or famous
or fashionably thin or comfortably fat
or even as peculiar as misguided as
a Democrat
or even a Democrat

even then
see
if you have a cherry tree
and I see it
I will chop that cherry tree down
stomp the cherries
fill my mouth completely with the pits to
spit them into the Potomac
and I don't know why
it is
that I cannot tell a lie

but that's the truth.

Henry Taylor

During the Great Debates, he tried a joke
and nothing happened. For an instant, hatred
for everything he saw leapt from his eyes
to his mouth, and down his arm to one hand
the camera caught and held as it gripped something—
the lectern, a table's corner, I forget what—
which, had it been alive, he would have killed.

Margaret Gibson

TWO WOMEN AT JFK GRAVESITE

Sun begins on the harp of trees, on snow
that the storm shoved down in the dark.
A troop of boys runs by.

Somebody near us, muffled, says,
in Arlington National Cemetery
we used to sled down these roads
when we were young and the stones
here were stones merely where the dead
were, frozen together.

The buds on the tulip trees prick
as we splinter through the wind.
The flame is nearly level to the stone.
We do not let ourselves feel what others
report to feel
because somehow

the Greek house, the hill, the sky
of monuments dismay our love until
awe dies and with it cheap propriety.
The dead, we know, rot as immaculate
children run down the hills
holding their cold ears

and the storm is shouting miles up the river
dropping ice like bullets on the unsuspect.
The ironic flame chatters in the weather,
our innocence spreads like a city at his feet.
We have killed no man with hate
or with love.

Before the stone circle of a hero's words
a man plainly cries, thinking
how the sweet cheat of his fate
goes bankrupt here, how no body
not of any woman consoles the discrepancies
in his dreams.

The sun is face down in the distant river.
We pick our way back softly, shunning
heroes like ice, ignoring the hurt
ordinary men, numbers 31-623, 25
who alive might have wanted us
and a simple cupboard life

before the abstract truckled and cajoled
and they went down, stunned
like fallen children from their toys.

Greg Orfalea

KITE DAY AT THE WASHINGTON MONUMENT

Kites!

Kites!

Kites!

Cars are obsolete today.

Only the green shoulder of a new woman
and the wind
that knocks at lattices
clangs garbage cans and greets
the face like a sister frantic
in her first love

Kites!

Soaring bits of quilts   azure
and rising and pulling at string on string
run by fathers like packhorses
and mothers heavy with children

They tug and fly   tug and fly
till blood leaves the hand
and string unravels and ravels
them out   barely seen dots
at the end of the eye

—The square and devil-shaped and space-
shipped and good ole cross-bow
10¢ messages that Today Is
Sunday and the wind jostled
the lattices with spring
and blew the *welcome* mat off

the step and swept
a Campbell soup can down
the alley at a boy who had fallen
asleep on a comic against brick
piled like cranberries

and who grabbed the ole bunting
and scar sheets and twined
a tail-of-a-thousand-tails
and launched the tissue paper
like a Chinese dragon
upward   upward
but the tail is long and weighs
down full as the kite just lofts
a bit higher than the trees
when his egg-beater feet
run like hell the opposite way

And he is lost as all on this carousel
grassy hill
as the pop music and essence
of magnolia join the waltzing
wind that tosses these figures

Of generals senators
students and street cleaners
onto the soft green shoulder of this woman
undulation
across the Ellipse
from the Constitution

For all along the roadway
of white brick into the sky
are the shadows of looping
criss-crossing

Kites!
Kites!

Kites!

Biographical Notes

ARCHIBALD MacLEISH (born 1892) was awarded the first of two Pulitzer Prizes for poetry (he was awarded a third for drama) for his *Conquistador* in 1933 and the second for his *Collected Poems* in 1953. He was awarded the Bollingen Prize in Poetry jointly with William Carlos Williams in 1952. His *New and Collected Poems: 1917–1976* was published in 1976. He has served in Washington as Librarian of Congress and as Assistant Secretary of State.

HORACE GREGORY (born 1898) has edited a number of volumes and is the author of a large and distinguished body of work, poetry, literary studies and essays and translations. His first volume of poetry, *Chelsea Rooming House*, was published in 1930. Volumes of his collected poetry are *Poems: 1930–1940* (1941), *Selected Poems* (1951) and *Collected Poems* (1964). He was awarded the Bollingen Prize in Poetry in 1965. An autobiographical volume, *The House on Jefferson Street: A Cycle of Memories*, was published in 1971 and a volume of his collected essays, *Spirit of Time and Place*, in 1973.

ALLEN TATE (born 1899) published his first volume of poetry, *Mr. Pope and Other Poems*, in 1928. Volumes of his collected poetry include *Selected Poems* (1937), *Poems: 1922–1947* (1948) and *The Swimmers and Other Selected Poems* (1970). He is the author also of a number of volumes of literary studies and essays, a novel, and two biographies of Civil War figures, and he has edited a number of volumes. He served in Washington as Poetry Consultant to the Library of Congress in 1943–1944. He was awarded the Bollingen Prize in Poetry in 1957.

MAY MILLER (born 1900) is the author of *Into the Clearing* (1959), *Poems* (1962), *Not That Far* (1973), *The Clearing and Beyond* (1974) and *Dust of Uncertain Journey* (1975).

RUTH LECHLITNER (born 1901) is the author of *Tomorrow's Phoenix* (1937), *Only the Years* (1944), *The Shadow on the Hour* (1956) and *A Changing Season* (1973) and of two plays in verse.

LAWRENCE LEE (born 1903) is the author of a number of volumes of poetry, among them *Summer Goes On* (1933), *Monticello and Other Poems*

(1937), *The Tomb of Thomas Jefferson* (1940) and *The Cretan Flute* (1968), and of a volume of stories, *Cockcrow at Night* (1973).

KATIE LOUCHHEIM (born 1903) is the author of *With or Without Roses* (1966) and has a new volume of poems in preparation. She has served as Vice Chairman ("that was before they invented Vice Chairperson") of the Democratic National Committee and as Deputy Assistant Secretary of State.

BREWSTER GHISELIN (born 1903) is the author of *Against the Circle* (1946), *The Nets* (1955) and *Country of the Minotaur* (1970) and is the editor of *The Creative Process* (1952).

RICHARD EBERHART (born 1904) is the author of a number of volumes of poetry. His first, *A Bravery of Earth*, was published in 1930. Volumes of his collected poems include *Selected Poems* (1951), *Collected Poems: 1930–1960* (1960), *Selected Poems: 1930–1965* (1965), for which he was awarded the Pulitzer Prize for poetry in 1966, and *Collected Poems: 1930–1976* (1976). He served in Washington as Poetry Consultant to the Library of Congress in 1959–1961. He was awarded the Bollingen Prize in Poetry jointly with John Hall Wheelock in 1962.

ROBERT PENN WARREN (born 1905) has published eleven volumes of poetry, ten novels and a number of other volumes. He served in Washington as Poetry Consultant to the Library of Congress in 1944–1945. His *Promises: Poems 1954–1956* was awarded the Pulitzer Prize for poetry in 1958. (His novel *All the King's Men* was awarded the Pulitzer Prize for fiction in 1947.) In 1967 he received the Bollingen Prize in Poetry and in 1976 the Copernicus Award for lifetime achievement in poetry.

STANLEY KUNITZ (born 1905) is the author of *Intellectual Things* (1930), *Passport to the War* (1944), *Selected Poems: 1928–1958* (1958), for which he was awarded the Pulitzer Prize for poetry in 1959, and *The Testing Tree* (1971). He is the author also of a volume of essays, *A Kind of Order, a Kind of Folly* (1975). He served in Washington as Poetry Consultant to the Library of Congress in 1974–1976.

JOSEPHINE JACOBSEN (born 1908) is the author of *Let Each Man Remember* (1940), *For the Unlost* (1946), *The Human Climate* (1953), *The*

Animal Inside (1966) and *The Shade Seller: New and Selected Poems* (1974). She served in Washington as Poetry Consultant to the Library of Congress in 1971–1973.

SELDEN RODMAN (born 1908) has published six volumes of poetry, *Mortal Triumph* (1932), *Lawrence: The Last Crusade* (1937), *The Airmen* (1941), *The Revolutionists* (1942), *The Amazing Year* (1947) and *Death of the Hero* (1964). He has also edited anthologies of poetry and has published a number of books on the history, art and culture of the Caribbean and South America.

ELIZABETH BISHOP (born 1911) is the author of *North & South* (1946), *Poems: North & South – A Cold Spring* (1955), *Questions of Travel* (1965), *The Complete Poems* (1969) and *Geography III* (1976). She served in Washington as Poetry Consultant to the Library of Congress in 1949–1950 and was awarded the Pulitzer Prize for poetry in 1956.

JOSEPHINE MILES (born 1911) is the author of *Lines at Intersection* (1939), *Poems on Several Occasions* (1941), *Local Measures* (1946), *Prefabrications* (1957), *Poems: 1930–1960* (1960), *Kinds of Affection* (1967), *Fields of Learning* (1972) and *To All Appearances: Poems New and Selected* (1974). She has also published a number of scholarly literary studies.

ROBERT HAYDEN (born 1913) is the author of *A Ballad of Remembrance* (1962), *Selected Poems* (1966), *Words in the Mourning Time* (1970), *The Night-Blooming Cereus* (1972) and *Angle of Ascent: New and Selected Poems* (1973). He has served in Washington as Poetry Consultant to the Library of Congress in 1976–1977.

KARL SHAPIRO (born 1913) is the author of a number of volumes of poetry. His *V-Letter and Other Poems* (1944) was awarded the Pulitzer Prize for poetry in 1945. He served in Washington as Poetry Consultant to the Library of Congress in 1946–1947. Volumes of his collected poems are *Poems: 1940–1953* (1953) and *Selected Poems* (1969). He was awarded the Bollingen Prize in Poetry jointly with John Berryman in 1969. A volume of his collected criticism, *The Poetry Wreck: Selected Essays, 1950–1970*, was published in 1975.

71

MURIEL RUKEYSER (born 1913) is the author of a number of volumes of poetry, among them *Theory of Flight* (winning publication in the Yale Series of Younger Poets in 1935), *U. S. 1* (1938), *A Turning Wind* (1939), *Beast in View* (1944), *The Green Wave* (1948), *Elegies* (1949), *Selected Poems* (1951), *Body of Waking* (1958), *Waterlily Fire: Poems 1932–1962* (1962), *The Speed of Darkness* (1968), *Breaking Open* (1973) and *The Gates* (1976). She has also published biography, fiction and translations. She received the Copernicus Award for lifetime achievement in poetry in 1977.

WILLIAM STAFFORD (born 1914) is the author of *West of Your City* (1960), *Traveling through the Dark* (1962), *The Rescued Year* (1966), *Allegiances* (1970) and *Someday, Maybe* (1973). He served in Washington as Poetry Consultant to the Library of Congress in 1970–1971.

RANDALL JARRELL (1914–1965) published his earliest work (with that of John Berryman and others) in *Five Young American Poets* in 1940. He was the author of *Blood for a Stranger* (1942), *Little Friend, Little Friend* (1945), *Losses* (1948), *The Seven-League Crutches* (1951), *Selected Poems* (1955), *The Woman at the Washington Zoo* (1960), *The Lost World* (1965) and *The Complete Poems* (1969). He served in Washington as Poetry Consultant to the Library of Congress in 1956–1958. He was the author also of a novel, *Pictures from an Institution* (1954), and essays, children's books and translations.

JOHN BERRYMAN (1914–1972) was the author of a number of volumes of poetry, notable among them *Homage to Mistress Bradstreet* (1956) and successive volumes of *The Dream Songs*. His earliest work appeared (with that of Randall Jarrell and others) in *Five Young American Poets* in 1940 and in *Poems* (1942) and *The Dispossessed* (1948). He was the author also of a biography, *Stephen Crane* (1950). He published *77 Dream Songs* in 1964 and *His Toy, His Dream, His Rest: 308 Dream Songs* in 1968. He was awarded the Pulitzer Prize for poetry in 1965 and was awarded the Bollingen Prize in Poetry jointly with Karl Shapiro in 1969. A collected volume of *The Dream Songs* was published in 1969. Several posthumous volumes have been published.

ERNEST KROLL (born 1914) is the author of *Cape Horn and Other Poems* (1952), *The Pauses of the Eye* (1955), *Fifty Fraxioms* (1973) and *More Fraxioms* (1977).

FRANCIS COLEMAN ROSENBERGER (born 1915) has worked for many years in Washington as an attorney at the United States Senate and has edited a number of volumes.

EDWARD WEISMILLER (born 1915) is the author of *The Deer Come Down* (winning publication in the Yale Series of Younger Poets in 1936) and *The Faultless Shore* (1946) and of a novel, *The Sleeping Serpent* (1962). He teaches at George Washington University.

EUGENE McCARTHY (born 1916) is the author of a volume of poetry, *Other Things and the Aardvark* (1968), and of a number of volumes on government and public affairs. He served for ten years, from 1949 to 1959, as a Member of the United States House of Representatives from Minnesota and for twelve years, from 1959 to 1971, as a Member of the United States Senate from Minnesota.

CHARLES EDWARD EATON (born 1916) is the author of six collections of poetry, *The Bright Plain* (1942), *The Shadow of the Swimmer* (1951), *The Greenhouse in the Garden* (1956), *Countermoves* (1963), *On the Edge of the Knife* (1970) and *The Man in the Green Chair* (1977), and of three collections of short stories. He is working on a seventh volume of poetry and a fourth volume of short stories.

JOHN MALCOLM BRINNIN (born 1916) is the author of *The Garden Is Political* (1942), *The Lincoln Lyrics* (1942), *No Arch, No Triumph* (1945), *The Sorrows of Cold Stone* (1951), *Selected Poems* (1963) and *Skin Diving in the Virgins* (1970). He is the author also of a memoir, *Dylan Thomas in America* (1955), and studies of Gertrude Stein and William Carlos Williams.

CHARLES G. BELL (born 1916) is the author of *Songs for a New America* (1953, revised 1966) and *Delta Return* (1956, revised 1969). He has also published two novels, *The Married Land* (1962) and *The Half Gods* (1968), short stories and essays.

ROBERT LOWELL (born 1917) is the author of a number of volumes of poetry, the first, *Land of Unlikeness*, with an Introduction by Allen Tate, in 1944. His *Selected Poems* was published in 1976. He was awarded the Pulitzer Prize for poetry in 1947 for his *Lord Weary's Castle* (1946) and again in 1974 for *The Dolphin* (1973). He served in Washington as Poetry Consultant to the Library of Congress in 1947–1948. He received the Copernicus Award for lifetime achievement in poetry in 1974.

RADCLIFFE SQUIRES (born 1917) is the author of *Cornar* (1940), *Where the Compass Spins* (1951), *Fingers of Hermes* (1965), *The Light under Islands* (1967) and *Waiting in the Bone* (1973). He has also published literary studies of Robinson Jeffers, Robert Frost, Frederic Prokosch and Allen Tate.

WILLIAM JAY SMITH (born 1918) has published six volumes of poetry, the first, *Poems*, in 1947. He served in Washington as Poetry Consultant to the Library of Congress in 1968–1970. His *New & Selected Poems* was published in 1970 and *The Streaks of the Tulip: Selected Criticism* in 1972. He is the author also of children's books.

WILLIAM MEREDITH (born 1919) is the author of *Love Letters from an Impossible Land* (winning publication in the Yale Series of Younger Poets in 1944), *Ships and Other Figures* (1948), *The Open Sea and Other Poems* (1958), *The Wreck of the Thresher and Other Poems* (1964), *Earth Walk: New and Selected Poems* (1970) and *Hazard: The Painter* (1975).

REED WHITTEMORE (born 1919) is the author of a number of volumes of poetry. His first, *Heroes & Heroines*, was published in 1946, the most recent, *The Mother's Breast and the Father's House*, in 1974. He has also published essays and a biography of William Carlos Williams. He served in Washington as Poetry Consultant to the Library of Congress in 1964–1965 and as Literary Editor of *The New Republic* in 1969–1973. He teaches at the University of Maryland.

JOHN PAUKER (born 1920) is the author of *Yoked by Violence* (1949) and *Excellency* (1968) and is a playwright, translator and short story writer. He works in Washington with the United States Information Agency.

HOWARD NEMEROV (born 1920) has published a number of volumes of poetry, his first, *The Image and the Law*, in 1947. He served in Washington as Poetry Consultant to the Library of Congress in 1963–1964. His *Winter Lightning: Selected Poems* was published in 1968. He has also published novels, short stories and essays. A volume of his *Collected Poems* is scheduled for publication in 1977.

RICHARD WILBUR (born 1921) is the author of *The Beautiful Changes* (1947), *Ceremony* (1950), *Things of This World* (1956), for which he was awarded the Pulitzer Prize for poetry in 1957, *Poems: 1943–1956* (1957), *Advice to a Prophet* (1961), *The Poems of Richard Wilbur* (1963), *Walking to Sleep* (1969) and *The Mind-Reader* (1976). He has also published translations and has edited a number of volumes. He was awarded the Bollingen Prize in Poetry jointly with Mona Van Duyn in 1971.

LOUIS SIMPSON (born 1923) is the author of *The Arrivistes* (1949), *Good News of Death* (1955), *A Dream of Governors* (1959), *At the End of the Open Road* (1963), for which he was awarded the Pulitzer Prize for poetry in 1964, *Selected Poems* (1965), *Adventures of the Letter I* (1971), *North of Jamaica* (1972) and *Searching for the Ox* (1976). He is the author also of a novel and of critical studies and has edited *An Introduction to Poetry* (1967).

MAXINE KUMIN (born 1925) is the author of *Halfway* (1961), *The Privilege* (1965), *The Nightmare Factory* (1970), *Up Country* (1972), for which she was awarded the Pulitzer Prize for poetry in 1973, and *House, Bridge, Fountain, Gate* (1975). She is also a novelist and the author of books for children.

A. R. AMMONS (born 1926) is the author of *Ommateum* (1955), *Expressions of Sea Level* (1964), *Corsons Inlet* (1965), *Tape for the Turn of the Year* (1965), *Norfield Poems* (1966), *Selected Poems* (1968), *Uplands* (1970), *Briefings* (1971), *Collected Poems: 1951–1971* (1972) and *Sphere: The Form of a Motion* (1974). A new volume, *The Snow Poems*, is in preparation. He was awarded the Bollingen Prize in Poetry in 1975.

ROBERT BLY (born 1926) is the author of *Silence in the Snowy Fields* (1962), *The Light around the Body* (1967), *The Morning Glory* (1969), *The Teeth Mother Naked at Last* (1970), *Jumping Out of Bed* (1972), *Sleepers Joining Hands* (1973) and *Old Man Rubbing His Eyes* (1975). A new volume, *This Body Is Made of Camphor and Gopher Wood*, is scheduled for publication. He is the author also of a number of translations.

RODERICK JELLEMA (born 1927) is the author of *Something Tugging the Line* (1974). He teaches at the University of Maryland.

O. B. HARDISON (born 1928) is the author of *Lyrics and Elegies* (1958) and has a new volume of poems in preparation. He is Director of the Folger Shakespeare Library in Washington.

ROBERT DANA (born 1929) is the author of *My Glass Brother* (1957), *The Dark Flags of Waking* (1964), *Journeys from the Skin* (1966), *Some Versions of Silence* (1967) and *The Power of the Visible* (1971).

GARY SNYDER (born 1930) is the author of a number of volumes of poetry, among them *Riprap* (1959), *Myths and Texts* (1960), *Six Sections from Mountains and Rivers without End* (1965), *The Back Country* (1967), *Regarding Wave* (1970) and *Turtle Island* (1974). He was awarded the Pulitzer Prize for poetry in 1975.

LINDA PASTAN (born 1932) is the author of *A Perfect Circle of Sun* (1971), *On the Way to the Zoo* (1975) and *Aspects of Eve* (1975) and has a new volume, *The Five Stages of Grief*, scheduled for publication early in 1978.

GRACE CAVALIERI (born 1932) has published two chapbooks of poems and has contributed poems to a number of magazines.

JUNE JORDAN (born 1936) is the author of *Some Changes* (1971), *New Days* (1974) and other volumes. Her *Things I Do in the Dark: Selected Poetry* was published in 1977.

HENRY TAYLOR (born 1942) is the author of *Horse Show at Midnight* (1966), *Breakings* (1971) and *An Afternoon of Pocket Billiards* (1975). He teaches in Washington at American University.

MARGARET GIBSON (born 1944) has published four chapbooks of poems, has contributed poems and fiction to a number of magazines, and is co-editor of the volume *Landscape and Distance: Contemporary Poets from Virginia* (1975).

GREG ORFALEA (born 1949) has published poems in a number of magazines. He lived in Washington for four years as a student at Georgetown University and for a year as a newspaper reporter. A first volume of poetry, *Pictures at an Exhibition*, is scheduled for publication.

77